Old Wanlockhead

Alex F. Young

A carriage and pair coming up the Mennock Pass, or *Monk's Pass*, around 1910, with some two and a half miles remaining to Wanlockhead. For the lead industry, the road was less important than that through Leadhills and into Lanarkshire, created by the Highways and Turnpike Roads Act of 1755, and only in 1791 was this road built. It was a toll road, under the charge of the Fourth (Upper Nithsdale) District Turnpike Road Trustees, which was petitioned by the mine owners, Ronald Crawford, Meason & Co., that if the carts bringing coal from the Nith Valley to the smelters were allowed toll free (the charge being 3d for the horse and 3d for the cart) the mining company would maintain the road, and this was agreed.

Text © Alex F. Young, 2010.
First published in the United Kingdom, 2010,
by Stenlake Publishing Ltd.
Telephone: 01290 551122
www.stenlake.co.uk

ISBN 978 1 84033 492 0

Printed by Berforts, 17 Burgess Road, Hastings, TN35 4NR

Acknowledgements

Ian Black, Michael J A Black, Robert Cooper of the Grand Lodge of Antient, Free and Accepted Masons of Scotland, Gilmour Harris, Bill Hunter of Kays of Scotland, Lynn Johnson, Congregational Liaison Officer, Church of Scotland, Edinburgh, John Taylor of Kilmaurs, Morag Williams of Dumfriesshire and Galloway Natural History and Antiquarian Society, Alistair Scott and Gwen Smart of the Hidden Treasures Museum of Lead Mining, Wanlockhead.

Illustration Acknowledgements

Ian Black gave illustrations on pages 22, 23 & 48 (right), whilst the remainder came from the Hidden Treasures Museum of Lead Mining, Wanlockhead.

Bibliography

Statistical Account of 1791-1799, volume 6, County of Dumfries, Sanquhar.

Statistical Account of 1834-1845, volume 4, County of Dumfries, Sanquhar.

Robert Brown, *More About the Mines and Minerals of Wanlockhead and Leadhills*, Transactions Series 3, Volume 13 (1925-26), Dumfriesshire and Galloway Natural History and Antiquarian Society.

Sandie Keggans, *Transporting the Lead*, The Wanlockhead Museum Trust, 2004.

H Gilbert Nicol, *Families of Wanlockhead*, Locin Press, New York, 1999.

All About Wanlockhead, The Wanlockhead Museum Trust, 2004.

Introduction

Wanlockhead owes its existence to the rich veins of lead bearing ore in the ground beneath it, but it was the search for gold and silver that put it on John Ainslie's map of 1789.

In 1568 James Stewart (1531-1570), Earl of Moray and Regent to the infant King James VI, granted a 19 year licence to a Dutchman, or perhaps he was German, Cornelius de Vois, to prospect for gold across Scotland. He came, apparently, on the recommendation of Queen Elizabeth of England. There were known deposits in Sutherland, but Cornelius concentrated on the valleys of Clydesdale and Nithsdale and in the first month his workforce of 120 men found 8lb of gold in alluvial deposits around Wanlockhead. Cornelius de Vois disappears from the records and a decade later the search was in the hands of an Englishman, Bevis Bulmer, who concentrated his, successful, searches in the Ettrick Forest area.

Next, in 1675, came Sir James Stanfield (1600-1687) of New Mills near Haddington, but his search was not for gold but for lead. A Yorkshire-born clothing manufacturer, who had served as a colonel on the Parliamentary side in the Civil War of 1641-1651, he was backed by other investors. The consortium met with success, and despite the high costs of transporting timber for props, and coal for the smelting furnaces, returned a profit. His son, Philip, was executed at Edinburgh in 1688 for his murder. No information survives as to the number of men employed, although they were probably paid 4d (Scots) per day. Nor can we know where, or how, they were housed – stone built cottages were a long way off – hence the work may only have been carried out in summer. There followed a succession of entrepreneurial ventures – starting with Matthew Wilson in 1691, who worked Margaret's Vein (Straitsteps) - through the eighteenth and into the nineteenth century, with the area becoming a honeycomb of mining activity.

A window into the workings of the mines can be found in the New Statistical Account for Sanquhar Parish, written in 1835 by the Rev Thomas Montgomery. Over the previous 50 years £500,000 had been invested in the mines, from which 47,420 tons of lead had been raised. However, there was the ongoing problem of diminishing return. The 1,037 tons produced in 1809 had sold for £32 per ton, whilst the 461 tons refined in 1830 realised only £13 per ton, to pay a workforce of; 4 overseers and clerks, 154 miners, 12 washers (and 20 boys), 8 smelters, and 10 smiths, carpenters and engineers. The dramatic fall in price was due to the relaxation of duty on imported lead, considered by some to be better quality. The men were paid, every three months, through a bargains system ie based on the amount of ore raised, and averaged £20 per annum, working six hours per day, six days per week. This would have paid for basic commodities, at the company store, and at the end of each quarter most were in debt. The song *Sixteen Tons*, first recorded in 1946 by the U.S. country singer Merle Travis, sums it up - *You load sixteen tons, and what do you get? / Another day older and deeper in debt. / Saint Peter, don't you call me, 'cause I can't go, / I owe my soul to the company store …*

The period of successive leases held by Ronald Crawford, Meason & Company since 1755 was coming to an end and, perhaps, not before time. The Duke of Buccleuch, now the 5th Duke, Walter Montague Douglas Scott (1806-1884), had a number of applicants, but not satisfied with any, decided to take over the mines on his own account in 1842, trading as the Queensberry Mines Company. In celebration, the villagers held a gala on 19 August, for which the Duke provided the biscuits and wine. James Stewart was appointed manager and would double output in the coming decade. Born in the village in 1795, he had been an overseer with the Scots Mining Company at Leadhills, and lived on the 728 acre Auchentaggart Farm, off the Mennock Pass, with his wife Mary Barker, whom he had married in 1833, and their sons, Peter and Thomas Barker Stewart. On his death, in June 1871, Thomas succeeded him.

The first industrial improvement Stewart tackled was the building of a new smelt mill, at a cost of £6,879 and the construction of a fume condenser, consisting of flues running up the hillside, costing £3,000. The flue system would recover up to 6% of the lead lost to the atmosphere. The Duke built a school and many new houses.

One problem for the lead industry, and indeed for villagers, was that of isolation. The bulk of the lead produced was exported through Leith and at one time the fifty mile route through Biggar was carrying 4,000 carts, each way, per annum. The road through the Mennock Pass was impassable until much later, when it carried industrial coal from Kirkconnel. The lead industry was at a very low ebb at the time of the inquiry into bringing the railway from Elvanfoot, and although it had little input, it would be a future beneficiary.

The last, successful, venture came in 1905 when Archibald and William Fraser of the Pumpherston Oil Company took up the lease of the mines, trading as the Wanlockhead Lead Mining Company. Their parents had been born in Wanlockhead, but the brothers were of Shotts in Lanarkshire. With five other partners, they invested £25,000 and took on John Mitchell as manager. Production concentrated at the Glencrieff vein, and with the introduction of modern machinery, output increased. The viability of the mining was based not only on the amount of ore extracted, but the cost of processing it and the market price of the end product. In 1914, 114 miners and 78 surface workers produced 3,234 tons of ore, but by 1918 production had fallen to 1,715 tons. In 1914 it cost £7.48 to produce a ton of lead, and

by 1918, £22.55, however in this same period its market value had only risen by £9 to £29. The break came in 1927 when the previous year's profits fell from £15,110 to a loss of £597. In 1928 the smelter closed and on 16 July 1931 mining operations ceased. The long era was over. The 1951 venture by Rio Tinto and others staggered through the 1950s, and died on the vine.

But it was not the end of Wanlockhead. The village recognised that the mining industry's days were over, but the thoughts of many turned to preserving the buildings and artefacts that were left. The height of their efforts coincided with a visit by the coal mining engineer, Geoff Downs Rose, on a recruiting drive for miners for the English Midlands. He picked up on the interest and enthusiasm, and laid the foundations of the Wanlockhead Museum Trust, built on a £10.00 grant from the village council. Evolution took care of the rest.

The view from Dod Hill with the Mennock Pass road coming in from the top right, passing the gamekeeper's cottage, on the open ground on its left, the railway station on its right, then Fraser Terrace and the Co-operative building. Old Library Row stands on the right of the view above the Duke's House, with Mennock View closest to the photographer, and St John's Church manse beyond the trees to the left.

The view down the Wanlock Valley, with Fraser Terrace in the foreground and the roof of the Co-op building just showing above. The Fraser Memorial Institute is on the right and through the break in the trees, the Duke's House. Both Fraser Terrace and the Institute date from the early twentieth century when the Fraser brothers', Wanlockhead Mining Company took over the mining lease.

With the blacksmith's premises in the foreground, the paths lead up to the higher ground on the left bank of the Wanlock Water. On the right is Old Library Row, its name dating its origins to the eighteenth century, when the library was housed in the thatched cottage. The two white cottages on the left are Greenbank Cottages and on the hillside, Hass Cottage.

The blacksmith William Shankland working on a horseshoe in the Smiddy (now the visitor centre) around 1900. His assistant is not known. Born at Thornhhill in 1837, Shankland married 19 year old Barbara Gibson at Sanquhar in January 1857, and by the spring of 1861 they were living in Church Street, Wanlockhead with two year old Jane and one year old Martha – their 21 month old son, John, had died in 1858. They later moved to the Old Manse and later again to Lilac Bank Cottage, before Goldscaur Row, where William was also the post master. He died of emphysema on 27 January 1913 and was buried in the village cemetery. Barbara died in March 1915. In the winter of 1788, the poet Robert Burns called at the village and, through the influence of a John Taylor, had a farrier/blacksmith, 'frost' or sharpen the points on the shoes of his horse, Pegasus. He paid for the work with the poem, *Pegasus at Wanlockhead*, written in Ramsay's Inn, whilst he waited for the work to be done; *Ye Vulcan's sons of Wanlockhead, / Pity my sad disaster! / My Pegasus is poorly shod / I'll pay you like my master*. Such was Burns' fame, that this was acceptable.

Wanlockhead Co-operative Society's premises in 1971, its centenary year, shortly before its closure. Its predecessor, the 'company store', had been run by mine manager, James Stewart, but on his death, in 1871, the Duke of Buccleuch handed it over to his workers, who formed it as a co-operative. It sold groceries, drapery, boots & shoes and coal, and by 1891, was dividing an annual profit of £952 amongst its 329 members, on sales of £6,206. By 1932, the falling workforce reduced its membership to 264, and in 1951 to 180 and its viability was in doubt. It joined the Scottish Co-operative Wholesale Society in 1959, but the decline continued and it ceased trading in 1971. Agnes Lucas, the manageress, bought the business and continued to trade for a time until forced to close, when the building was demolished.

The date stone from the Co-op building, set into the ground where it had stood.

Agnes Lucas (1918-1990), George McCall (1903-1982) and Nancy Laidlaw in the Co-op store in 1964. Thought to have come from Glasgow, Agnes managed the store for the Co-op until taking it over, on her on behalf, in 1971. George drove the shop's delivery van and was a coal merchant and undertaker on his own behalf. Nancy left the village soon after to settle in Bo'ness, West Lothian.

The Fraser Memorial Institute, with part of the school showing to the left, was designed by the Hawick based architect James Pearson Alison (1862-1932) and built by the Edinburgh contractor Thomas Topping (sequestrated in June 1930). Opened in December 1908, it was gifted to the village by the Fraser brothers; John (1851-1944) of the Glasgow iron and steel merchants, Messrs Robertson & Fraser of West George Street, and William (1853-1915) and Archibald (1857-1951) of the Pumpherston Oil Company, West Lothian. They were born at Shotts, Lanarkshire, and gifted the hall in memory of their parents John and Isabella Fraser, nee Milligan, who were natives of Wanlockhead. In 1906 Archibald and William had taken over the lease on the New Glencrieff mine, founding the Wanlockhead Lead Mining Company. The Institute's concrete structure consisted of a reading room, billiard room, a smoking room and baths, under a 300 seat capacity hall (47 feet by 25 feet) and caretaker's accommodation – occupied for sometime, initially, by George McCall. The management trustees consisted of the mine manager, the two ministers, the schoolmaster and four workers. Its ferro-concrete type structure may have been the latest in 1900s building technology but therein lay its weakness. It was closed in 1964 and demolished as a dangerous building. It was literally falling to pieces. The memorial plaque on the end wall was set into the ground where it had stood, and was landscaped by the BBC's 'Beechgrove Garden' programme in 1997.

Dressed in their blue sashes and gold trimmed aprons, members of lodge Wanlock No. 1187, of the Freemasons, on the rear stairway of the Fraser Memorial Institute on 3 July 1919. Founded in May that year, it would disband in 1935 due to falling membership as a result of declining employment and the drift of men and their families from the village. The following have been named. Front flanks (left and right), bearing swords, Thomas Templeton (Inner Guard) and Hugh Mitchell (Tyler). First row; George L Parson (Senior Warden), James Mitchell, in the top hat (Right Worshipful Master) and William Mitchell (Junior Warden). Second row, John Nelson (Senior Deacon), Nicolas Penrose (Chaplain) and Andrew Allison (Junior Deacon). In the top row, Adam McKean is on the left and William Boyd (Past Master) is on the right.

From the late eighteenth century, no wedding or curling *bon spiel*, was complete without the village band, photographed here outside the school in the 1890s. Their instruments had been presented by the Duke of Buccleuch in 1871 at a cost of £90 (£46,267.35 in 2009) and were replaced in 1911. In 1926 it won the Fourth Class Championship Shield of the Scottish Amateur Brass Band Association, but with declining employment in the village, members were leaving and in 1935 the committee called in the instruments and uniforms. Two attempts were made to re-constitute it, the first in 1946, and the second in 1962, when there was a proposal to form a joint band with Leadhills. Neither came to fruition and the instruments were later sold to Leith Band. In 2009 one of the tubas turned up in an antique shop, and is now back in Wanlockhead where, one of the cornets has also re-appeared.

Wanlockhead Amateur Dramatic Society on stage, in the Fraser Institute, with what is thought to be a 1950s production of the Fife miner-playwright Joe Corrie's (1894-1968), four act Scots comedy, *Kye Amang the Corn*. From left to right the players are; Betty Cowal, Eddie Foley, Jimmy Young, Nancy Gilchrist, Jackie Syme, Jimmy Russell and Isobel Murray. Some have suggested it may have a been *Cock of the North*, but with all of the players now having passed away, confirmation is difficult.

The school, consisting of three classrooms divided by folding partitions, was gifted by the Duke of Buccleuch when he took over the mining interests in 1842. The 1841 Census shows the village teacher as 40 year old, Dumfriesshire born, Thomas Lorimer, who was succeeded by 21 year old, Glaswegian John McArthur, who came with his sister Margaret as his housekeeper. An advertisement in *The Scotsman* of 14 December 1850 announces – *Just out, price 3d., The Arithmeticon; or Inexhaustible Book of Exercises in the Simple Rules of Arithmetic, by J M'Arthur, Teacher, Wanlockhead*. Mr McArthur was replaced in 1856 by Mr Gilbert Dawson (1828-1908), who served until 1882 when he was succeeded by John Edmond. The slates in foreground were from the Fraser Memorial Institute, demolished in the winter of 1964-65.

Pupils at the school in 1926 when the roll of 36 was made up of 19 girls and 17 boys - some shod in hobnail boots. The only two remembered today are in the third row from the front – on the right is Jenny Arrigoni of Glencrieff Cottages, and, two along from her, Peggy Mitchell, who lived on Goldscaur Row. Seven years later the roll would rise to over 100 pupils and four teachers but declined over the years until its closure in 1976, when the 11 remaining pupils transferred to Leadhills Primary School.

The view south, around 1904, taking in the Curfew Bell with the stable for the Co-op's horse to the left, and the east end of New Row and the railway station near the skyline, to the right. In 1911, the hillside above New Row would be the site of Fraser Terrace. Little information survives on the Curfew Bell, although a similar one in neighbouring Leadhills dates from 1777. The word 'curfew' derives from the French *couvre feu* - covering of the fire – an important nightly precaution in thatched roof houses. Thomas Gray's *Elegy Written in a Country Churchyard* opens with the lines; *The curfew tolls the knell of parting day* ... but that was in a village with a church and a bell tower – having neither, Wanlockhead, and Leadhills made do with bells in frameworks. Within living memory it was used at funerals, being rung a quarter of an hour before the service, to summon the mourners, and continued until the cortege was out of sight on its a way to the cemetery. It was taken down in the 1930s, the scrap metal putting money in the pocket of Billy Lowther, a travelling dealer.

The Rev Charles Patrick Blair's son, Patrick Charles Bentley Blair was a 2nd Lieutenant in the 5th Battalion of the Rifle Brigade when he was killed near Ypres on the night of Sunday, 6 July 1915, and buried at Talana Farm Cemetery (named for the 1899 Boer War battle, Talana Hill), near Boezinge in Flanders. Born at Wanlockhead on 18 July 1891, he was educated at Fettes College, Edinburgh, and Cambridge University, where he gained a 1st Class Classical Tripos. In sport, he played rugby – for his school, his university and, at least once, for his country, against France. Before joining the army, he served a short time with the Egyptian Civil Service.

The War Memorial has a six feet tall, battle dress clad, soldier fashioned in marble, with his rifle inverted, atop an eight feet high granite plinth, bearing the names of the 16 Wanlockhead men lost in the First World War. It was unveiled on Sunday, 16 September 1920, at a service conducted by the Rev Charles Patrick Blair (1859-1923), before a crowd nearing 1,000. Ironically the Rev Blair's son, Lieut. Patrick Charles Bentley Blair, is the first name. Two names were added after the Second World War – Sergeant Thomas McCall of the Royal Air Force and Corporal William Carmichael Wilson of the Kings Own Scottish Borderers.

Sergeant Thomas McCall of the Royal Air Force Volunteer Reserve, the 20 year old son of John and Mary McCall of Wanlockhead who was killed in action on 24 February 1944, and William Carmichael Wilson of the King's Own Scottish Borderers, who died in action near Gelderland on the Dutch / German border on 19 September 1944 were the only Wanlockhead casualties in the Second World War. Thomas was a Flight Engineer with 578 Squadron based at RAF Burn in Yorkshire, flying Handley Page Halifax III bombers. On the night of Thursday, 24 February his squadron joined a force of 554 Lancasters, 169 Halifaxes and 11 Mosquitoes on a bombing raid over the ball bearing factories at Schweinfurt in Bavaria, southern Germany. The raid was considered a success, with the loss of only 33 aircraft – 26 Lancasters and seven Halifaxes - including Thomas's, (LW503, call sign LK-Z) brought down over Abbeville in northern France, on its return. The six other crew members survived and were captured, but Thomas was killed. He was buried at Abbeville Communal Cemetery Extension and lies with 1,754 burials from the First World War and 347 from the Second World War.

Having started in the old schoolhouse in 1756, and moved to a cottage in what was later known as (Old) Library Row in 1788, the 112 members of the Miners' Library brought their stock of 2,000 books to this building in 1850. The library's president, William Weir, had prevailed upon the Duke of Buccleuch to grant ground for the building, and to engage his architect, Charles Howitt (1826-1875), then of Buccleuch Mains. Howitt was later responsible for Kirkconnel School House (1856), Drumlanrig Bridge (1860), Thornhill School (1864) and Penpont Parish Church (1867). The bronze wall plaque commemorates the poet Robert Reid, *Rob Wanlock*, son of the mining clerk John Reid, who was born in the village in 1850, emigrated to Canada in 1877. One of nature's poets – "he found his best themes in the lilt of the laverock, the wild cry of the whaup, and the brown heather". His first book, 'Moorland Rhymes' was published in 1874 at Dumfries. He died at Montreal in 1922.

Left: Certificate No. 167, issued to William Meickle (Meikle) on being admitted a member of Wanlockhead's *Society for Purchasing Books*, on Wednesday, 7 January 1829. Little is known of Meikle, but he may have been the blacksmith husband of Janet Wyllie. Of the other names on the certificate, Thomas Hislop, was clerk to the Society from 1822 until 1830, having joined in 1814, whilst President John Lorimer had been a member since 1812. On 26 February 1901 this certificate was transferred to James Gass, a 37 year old lead miner living at Townhead Cottages with his 34 year old Lugar born wife Grace. Initially, the annual subscription was 4/- (20p) per annum, halving to 2/- (10p) in 1783 and only rising again to 4/- in 1921. By 1790 they had acquired 309 books, rising to 1,050 in 1829, 1,909 by 1848 and 3,116 in 1901.

Right: The library was founded on 1st November 1756 – 15 years after the Leadhills Reading Society – with a membership of 30, but it is not clear when they first used bookplates, or who engraved the copper printing plate, still held by the museum. The motto *God Send Grace* comes from the Crichton family of Sanquhar Castle, and the hands of friendship and the choice of an ore bucket, hammer, pick and shovel is obvious. This particular label, No. 1769, relates to volume two of the five volume set, *Travels in Poland, Russia, Sweden and Denmark – illustrated with charts and engravings*, by William Coxe, Rector of Bemerton, and printed by T Cadell and W Davies in London's Strand. It was 'Presented to The Wanlockhead Library by his Grace The Duke of Buccleuch & Queensberry, 1844'.

Jimmy Jamieson with the Co-op van, and 'Roger' the horse, outside the Old Post Office on Goldscaur around 1935 with, perhaps, his wife.

The view down Goldscaur Row (*gold* and *scaur*, a steep, eroded hill) around 1900. The house beyond the two-storey building, was the home of the blacksmith William Shankland who was also the postmaster. By 1920 the thatched roofs were replaced with slate and the last two cottages had second storeys added. Only in 1951 was it supplied with electricity.

Archie Robertson and his eight year old son Glen, with Ian Black of Mooredge Cottages, clearing a path through the snow in the early 1960s. Archie, a native of Newcastle, was employed on Buccleuch Estates, running a small firewood business at weekends. After Second World War service with the Royal Navy – including involvement in the D-Day Landings - Ian Black joined the Ministry of Transport and Civil Aviation (Civil Aviation Authority from 1972) as a technician, and was at this time employed at Lowther Hill, later going to Turnhouse, Edinburgh and Prestwick.

Mary Black (nee McLellan) coming from the horse-powered Wanlockhead Co-op van, previously used by Dalziel Co-op Society in Motherwell, in the 1950s. What was not on the van today, would be there for her tomorrow. Born in Dumfries, she married Ian Black (see previous page), going with him around the country on his CAA postings. She died in August 1973 at the early age of 42.

WANLOCKHEAD, SHOWING "LOTUS LODGE" HIKERS' HOSTEL.
1,400 FEET ABOVE SEA LEVEL.

Lotus Lodge (centre), with the top end of Goldscaur Row on the left, and Wanlock House and Mennock to the right. In the foreground are Long Row and the course of the Wanlock Water as it makes its way down the valley to join the Crawick Water above Spango Bridge and flow into the River Nith above Sanquhar.

Lotus Lodge shortly after its opening by the Scottish Youth Hostel Association on 4th July 1936. Thought to have been a Buccleuch Estate shooting lodge, it was home to Dr John Wilson, until his death on 26 June 1905 (interred at Duddingston Parish Kirk, Edinburgh), and then John Kerr (appointed a Justice of the Peace in April 1912), a mines overseer, until his death on 25 February 1932, when it was bought by the SYHA. It was their 53rd hostel, and the fourth to be opened that year, accommodating 40 'hikers' under the care of its warden Adam Phillips, a native of Joppa, Edinburgh. The opening was performed by Mr H E Gladstone of Capenoch, Thornhill, Convener of Dumfriesshire County Council, and during the ceremony, a telegram was sent to Fordie Lodge at Comrie in Perthshire, one of the other hostels opened that day. The 1881 Census lists the building as "Surgeon's House", and hence, perhaps, it was Dr Wilson who named it 'Lotus Lodge', bringing to mind, the Pictish king, Lothus.

The 325 seat Church of St John 'a buttressed box of harled rubble, with hood-moulded, pointed windows', on Church Street, in the early 1900s. It was built in 1848-49 by John Douglas (1798-1853), Clerk of Works of Drumlanrig Mains, at a cost between £70 and £80, to Walter Francis, Duke of Buccleuch, who also granted Carcoside Farm and Orchard Farm (where in early times there had been a religious house for women) for its support. Its predecessor, termed a 'preaching station', with 250 seats, dated from 1755. One third of the minister's stipend of £65 came from the mine owners and the remainder from miners earning more than 1/- per day, who contributed 4/- per annum. An 1836 ecclesiastical survey found the population of 716 was made up of 678 churchmen (no mention of women or children), 24 dissenters and 14 nondescripts. On 27 January 1861 Wanlockhead became a *quoad sacra* parish and was disjoined from Sanquhar. Its first minister, James Laidlaw (1801-1887), a native of Cummertrees in Dumfriesshire, served until 1886 when he handed over to the Rev Charles Patrick Blair. Its 1891 communion roll stood at 140 but over the years this declined and in 1985 the building was sold to the trustees of the Wanlockhead Museum for £500.

A 1960s photograph of Church Street, blanketed with the previous night's snow. Nineteenth century reports speak of drifts covering the houses, but in recent years the total would not exceed two feet, falling over 29 winter days.

The Gracie family outside the church on Church Street in the summer of 1949. Crouched at the front are Robert Coltart Gracie (b.1927), newly demobbed from the army, his sister Agnes (with Glen the dog) and cousin Robert Coulson. Standing in the centre is Robert and Agnes's mother, Annie, whilst their father, Thomas stands at the right. On the left is Uncle William Coltart with Aunt Jessie Coltart beside him and their twin sons Thomas and Andrew at the back. Second from the right is Alice Stevenson, a friend of Uncle William and Aunt Jessie.

Retired master joiner Robert Brown in the family home in George Square, behind which was his workshop – the circular saw powered by a bull-nosed Morris motor car engine. Born on 7 July 1864 to Ann Brown, he married 29 year old Elspeth Moffat of Meadowfoot on New Year's Day, 1897. In this photograph he is flanked by his life's interests – books and rocks. As an amateur geologist he wrote many papers on the mines and minerals around Wanlockhead and Leadhills, and two of his papers, '*The Mines and Minerals of Leadhills*' (1919) and '*More About the Mines and Minerals of Wanlockhead and Leadhills*' (1926) were published by the Dumfriesshire and Galloway Natural History and Antiquarian Society. He lived all his life in Georges Square and died there in June 1941.

The residents of The Corner on Manse Road, and their children, turnout for a photographer in 1890s. As the exact date of the photograph is unknown they cannot be named but the first house from the left could have been home to Janet Milligan (b. 1850), her son John and daughter Mary. It was demolished in the 1950s. The two houses under the dark thatch – later converted to a two storey house with a £25 grant from the mining company - may have been home to the Watsons and the Slimmons, and in the quartet of women will be mother and daughter, Mary and Jessie Meikle. This house was demolished in 1912.

LILAC COTTAGE & BELTON HOUSE, WANLOCKHEAD.

Lilac Cottage, the larger, three house, Lily Bank row with its thatched roof, and Belton House to the right. Built in the late eighteenth century, possibly as a shooting lodge, Belton House was a two storey, three bay house before being added to in the late nineteenth century. It was home to the mine manager John Mitchell until his death in 1920.

The (United) Free Church and manse (later Hastings' House) around 1900. Following the 'Disruption' in the established Church of Scotland when, on 18 May 1843, over 450 ministers walked out of the church's General Assembly over the question of 'patronage' ie the right of each church's patron, in Wanlockhead's case the Duke of Buccleuch (Walter Francis, 5th Duke, 1806-1884), to appoint his choice of minister. Wanlockhead's minister, Thomas Hastings (1795-1875) was one of the dissenters and left the church with some 200 of his congregation. Across the country the emerging the industrial middle class financed the building of 470 new, 'Free Church of Scotland' church buildings within a year, but not until 1851 did Wanlockhead have its own, a 'wooden kirk', built near the present bowling green, (demolished 1953), costing £149.10.8 – the Duke being somewhat tardy in granting them ground. In 1851 the congregation were allowed to build a manse (demolished in 1953) and, finally, in 1859, a stone built church. At the rear of the manse is the Co-op bakery horse drawn van and driver.

Above: High House Row, on the hillside above Lilybank, were the highest inhabited houses in Scotland, of which only the centre section survives. For many years through the 1880s and 1890s (when they were known as part of Townhead) they were occupied by William Lorimer and his family and the McCall family. In 1942, as part of the 'Recording Scotland Project' aimed at depicting scenes, buildings and ways of life threatened by war, they were painted by the Scottish watercolourist Anna Dixon, RSW (1873-1959).

Left: The hamlet of Meadowfoot, in the shadow of Sowen Dod, in the 1890s, with the Wanlock Water passing on the valley floor. The 12 cottages had almost 50 occupants, ranging in age from infants to 70 year olds, and although most were employed in lead mining - miners, refiners, engine keepers, lead washers and smelters - it was also home to William Mitchell, the co-op store manager, Alexander Wilson, a 13 year old assistant grocer, and Alexander Sharpe, a shepherd. They were then owned by Buccleuch Estate but, by the 1930s most were owned by their occupiers.

THE MEADOWFOOT, WANLOCKHEAD.

The view across the valley of the Wanlock Water from Shieling Rig, with Meadowfoot, the settling ponds and the old cemetery, where the first interment was that of 10 month old William Philip, who died on 2 April 1751, under the shadow of Sowen Dod (1791 feet) and Wanlock Dod (1807 feet), separated by Whyte's Cleuch, and the Bay Mine, which was worked until around 1900. The settling ponds, used to remove lead from the sludge, were finally drained in 1957 and the lead recovered.

A family on a Sunday outing prospecting for gold with a sluice box in the Wanlock Water below the ruins of the Crushing Mill around 1917. The mill, and its 28 feet diameter water driven wheel, seen here, dates from 1842 when the mines were taken over by the Duke of Buccleuch. The ore was brought by narrow gauge railway, or tramway, along the upper level on the right, from the Bay Mine, and dropped into the 'bins' to keep each 'bargain' or gang of miners produce seperate for payment, before passing through the crushing process and taken, again by tramway, to the smelter. It was in use until the building of the new mill at New Glencrieff in 1911.

Miners in front of the pumping house at the Daisy Bell shaft – capable of raising 72 gallons of water per minute – with their bowler-hatted manager, John Mitchell (1853-1920), who had been appointed superintendent when the Wanlockhead Lead Mining Company was founded by William and Archibald Fraser in 1906. All, but one, have a tallow lamp hooked into their hats – no hard hats in those days. The small brass, coffee pot shaped, lamp consisted of a hooked handle, a hinged lid and a spout for the wick was an improvement on the candle, although the carbide lamp was just around the corner. Some have their chisels, also known as moils or jumpers, tied up with rope, used to drive holes for blasting. Pneumatic drills would not come until 1912-13. The name 'Daisy Bell' comes from the popular song about a tandem bicycle, 'a bicycle built for two' written in 1892 by the English songwriter Harry Dacre.

Three engineers, with samples of Galena bearing rock, photographed at the re-opening of the New Glencrieff Mine in the early 1950s. In 1951 the Siamese Tin Syndicate Ltd, Bangrin Tin Ltd, and Rio Tinto started operations at Glencrieff, but it came to nothing, Rio Tinto pulling out in 1954 and the others in 1959. Standing is Jimmy Stewart, whilst crouched in front are a German engineer, whose name cannot be recalled, Peter Slimmon and William Syme. With no dangerous gasses underground carbide lamps, as Jimmy Stewart wears, were safe.

A group of men installing the power cable to the submersible pump at level 8 (955 feet) of Glencrieff Mine around 1952. Drainage work continued until it reached over 900 feet and faltered. Following the line of the cable, the men are; Charlie Shambrook, Willie Cummins, Hugh Nelson, Alistair Scott, John Smillie, Alex McCall, Robert Howland, John Wilson and Antonio Tonnetti. Behind them is the engineering workshop and to its left Charlie Shambrook's car.

The smelter beyond Meadowfoot around 1910, with 'lead pigs' ready for dispatch. It was built in the 1840s, at a cost of £6,879, and the underground flue running up the hill, to capture lead in the exhaust fume, added a few years later at a cost of £3,000. The process was overhauled by the Frasers when they took over in 1906, and now consisted of two roasting furnaces, five Scotch Ore Hearths and one slag hearth. Other changes included the scrapping of the de-silvering and refining plants. Operations ceased with the onset of the Depression in the early 1930s and, with what had value as scrap stripped out, the building served as an artillery practice target in the Second World War.

Wanlock Lads football team around 1938, with: Front row (left to right); Harry Keggans, David Graham, John Dalling, Eddie Inglis, unknown. Back row; David Young, Wull Laidlaw, Stanley West, Jimmy McMurdo, Willy Anderson and Willy McDowall. Founded in 1909 they played in the Dumfries Juvenile League until 1948, with a season in the Juniors before joining Dumfries & District Amateur Football League. It was disbanded at the end of the 1980-81 season, coming second bottom of the 2nd Division. Having played 22 games, they had 3 wins, 3 draws and 16 defeats.

Employees of Robert McAlpine & Sons of Glasgow photographed, with the construction locomotive – an 0.4.0 saddletank locomotive built by Hudswell Clarke of the Old Railway Foundry, Leeds – during the building of the line from Elvanfoot. This one is said to be works No. 522, delivered to McAlpine in March 1899, but enough of the lettering on the boiler is visible to suggest the name *Trent*, whilst No. 522 was named *Covenanter* by McAlpine – they bought 10 of this model in 1899-1900. The name Trent was used on locomotives of the Trent Iron Works at Frodingham in Lincolnshire – could McAlpine have hired one of theirs, and brought it north with the track?

The railway station, with the village spread along the valley below, in the 1900s. The locomotive, No. 172 of the Caledonian Railway who operated the line, was an 0-4-4T, built at their St Rollox Works in Glasgow in 1884, and would operate here until replaced in 1925. After many years of lobbying, the Light Railway Commissioners, on behalf of the Board of Trade, held a one day public enquiry at Leadhills on Wednesday, 14 April 1897, where the Caledonian Railway presented its case for building a 7 mile, 5 furlong and 2 chain line from their station at Elvanfoot to Leadhills and Wanlockhead. Authorisation was granted with the order - Caledonian Railway (Leadhills and Wanlockhead Light Railway) Order, 1898. The line opened to Leadhills on 1 October 1901 and to Wanlockhead on the anniversary, a year later. It closed on 31 December 1938.

Members of the Wanlockhead Curling Society, with their trophies, in 1912;

Front row (left to right); Wull Carmichael, unknown, William Jamieson, BEM, unknown, Robert Dalziel, Wull Mitchell (mine manager), Harry Edwards (Schoolmaster), Robert Brown, Wull Kerr, John Laidlaw, James Gass, Davy Jamieson (Scapper).

Middle row; Geordie Gracie, John Coltart, (?) Coltart, Geordie Watson, Jock Wilson, Archie Mitchell, Johnnie Murray, Jimmy Kerr, Charlie McMillan, Willie Wilson (?), unknown and Jimmy Jamieson.

Back row; Will McMillan, Jimmy McCall, John Dalziel, unknown, Andrew Coltart, Jimmy Paterson (?), John Gilchrist, Tam Coltart, Charlie Harkness, Harry Edward.

As can be seen by the trophies, this had been a particularly successful year for the club having won the trophies displayed at the front. – possibly the Nithsdale Bowl, unknown, The Dewar Shield, Waterlow (Dumfriesshire) Cup, Fraser Cup and unknown. It is not known when the 'roaring game' was first played at Wanlockhead but when the Society was founded on 26 December 1777 it had 123 members. It finally closed in 1944.

Thomas Gilchrist of Wanlockhead Curling Society and his team, photographed as the first winners of the Dewar Challenge Shield in 1913. The shield had been presented to the Society the previous year by Sir Thomas R Dewar (1864-1930), 1st Baron Dewar, of the Scotch whisky distillers and blenders. His travels around the world, promoting the company's whisky, can be plotted - where you find a 'Dewar Shield', having travelled as far as Fiji. His introduction to Wanlockhead probably came about through being on a grouse shoots as guest to the Duke of Buccleuch. His other legacy is said to be his 'Dewarisms' – *When a man says his word is as his bond – get his bond, Never invest in a going concern until you know which way it is going, We have a great regard for old age when it is bottled* and *A teetotaller is one who suffers from thirst instead of enjoying it.* Thomas Gilchrist won the Shield again in 1922, and the last winner was David Jamieson in 1930, whose name also appears against 1916, 1920 and 1929. The trophy is now in the care of the Museum.

Boys of Wanlockhead School Curling Club around 1910. The club was founded at a meeting called by Mr John Edmond, headmaster, (president of the Wanlockhead Curling Society, 1889-1920) on 10 November 1883 and had an initial membership of 18, paying 3d. to join, and an annual fee of 2d. The uniqueness of a 'boys' curling club aroused the interest of the Royal Caledonian Curling Club in 1908, and this photograph may be a copy of one it requested. In 1910 the membership stood at 27, but due to a combination of milder winters, when there was insufficient ice, and waning interest, it finished in 1951. On the right of the centre row is Harry Edmond, the headmaster's son (b.1898), who was the first winner of the Fraser Rose Bowl, gifted by Archibald Fraser in 1913. A native of Carnbee, Anstruther, Fife, John Edmond came to Wanlockhead in 1881-82, and married Grace Gibb Gillespie at Auchterderran, Fife in 1887. They had three children, George, Barbara and Harry.

The School Curling Club on the ice, thought to be the pond at Peter's Sike Head, across the railway line and opposite the Free Church manse. It is not known who Peter was, but a *sike* or *syke* is a small stream or water course, especially one in a hollow or on flat boggy ground. As in photographs of their adult counterparts, it has not possible to identify the source of the stone. Due its almost perfect granite – its small crystals making it less likely to chip – the island of Ailsa Craig in the Firth of Clyde has been the most popular, but stone from other quarries around the country have been used. The nearest to Wanlockhead would have been Craighead Quarry at Crawfordjohn, from 1851. Its stone is black with creamy coloured crystals, but much more brittle.

Margaret 'Peggy' Gemmell as an 85 year old, and one of Wanlockhead's oldest residents, in 1904. The daughter of John Laidlaw, a lead miner, and his wife Agnes Thomson, she was born at Leadhills in 1819 and married Andrew Gemmell, a lead miner-cum-grocer on 20 March 1841. By the time of the 1851 Census they were living at No. 15, 3 Fourth Row, Wanlockhead with their children; David (9 years), Agnes (7 years) and John (nine months). Another window is the Census Return of 1881, when Margaret was living in Manse Street, Sanquhar, with Agnes now 38 years and still unmarried, Andrew a 24 year old lead smelter, Thomas, aged 22 years and working as a lead mines labourer and 19 year old Jane. On the night of the Census (Sunday, 3 April), Andrew was with his cousin, George Morran at Ednum Hill Farm, Annan. Andrew died, of bronchitis, on 28 December 1882, leaving Margaret a widow until her death aged 96 years, at a quarter past midnight on the morning of Monday, 22 February 1915. Her death was registered by Mary Johnstone, nurse, of 4 Argyle Park Terrace, Edinburgh.

THE "PHEASANT" TREE

This Tree was planted in 1884
By Walter Scott,
Lead-Miner, Wanlockhead.

A Novel Work of Art. to be seen at
the quiet little village of Wanlockhead.
So perfect and life like is the appearance
of the work that controversy has frequently
arisen amongst visitors as to the reality of the
"Pheasant. Thousands of visitors have called
And seen the Tree.

Retired lead miner Walter Scott and his 'Pheasant Tree' shrub, in his garden at Glencrieff Cottages, around 1900 – by 1901 he and his wife Marion had moved to Straitsteps. Such were Scott's topiary skills that the shrub, planted in 1884, brought him to the notice of post card producers and the *Hamilton Herald* which described the work as – *a specimen of arboriculture which is in every way unique.* Born in the village on 3 May 1843 to Walter and Elizabeth Scott, he married Catherine Taylor (1840-1875) in 1863 and Marion Templeton (1835-1909) in 1878. His death certificate shows that he died at Wanlockhead on 13 April 1918, aged 73 years, of chronic bronchitis and heart failure, and that he was then married to Ann McLean – a marriage which does not appear in the register of marriages.

Below: The Radio Station on Lowther Hill shortly after building work was completed by the Ministry of Transport in 1948. Digging foundations, a workman found a human skull and a stone bearing the inscription, 'WK 1767 E 25', the first of 14 to be uncovered as the work progressed. Naturally, the National Air Traffic Control Service were more interested in the future than the past and were unaware the hill top had been the burial place of eighteenth century suicides. This initial find was interpreted as; *WK* - the deceased's initials, the year 1767 and *E* for Aetat ie. age, 25 years. In his 1876 book *The Enterkin*, John Brown relates one of the burials; *One can imagine the miserable procession as it slunk, often during night, through the villages ... everyone turning from it as abhorred. Then, arrived at this high and desolate region, the horse was taken out, and the weary burden dragged with pain up to its resting place, and carried head foremost as in despite; then a shallow hole dug, and the long uncouth box pushed in – the cart and harness left to rot.*

Right: Logan Marr, a National Air Traffic Control Service's technician, leaving the Radio Station on Lowther Hill (2378 feet) to return to Wanlockhead, a mile and a half and some 900 feet below, after completing his 48 hour shift. A native of the village, he joined the NATCS in 1954 from his National Service with the Royal Air Force and was at Lowther Hill for a time. Between 1948 and 1968, Lowther was the master station of the Scottish Gee-Chain (*Gee* being a codename rather than an acronym), with slaves at Great Dun Fell in Cumberland, Craigowl Hill near Dundee and Rhu Staffnish in Argyll, which controlled transatlantic civil air traffic from the north of England as far as 10 degrees west.

Logan died at his home in Stewarton, Ayrshire in February 2010.